SURVIVE
MOUNTAINS

D0840856

SURVIVE
MOUNTAINS

JUSTIN LICHTER

FALCONGUIDES

GUILFORD, CONNECTICUT
HELENA, MONTANA

FALCONGUIDES ®

An imprint of Rowman & Littlefield
Falcon and FalconGuides are registered trademarks and Make
Adventure Your Story is a trademark of Rowman & Littlefield.

Distributed by NATIONAL BOOK NETWORK

Copyright © 2016 by Rowman & Littlefield

Photos and illustrations by Justin Lichter, unless otherwise noted.

British Library Cataloguing-in-Publication Information available

Library of Congress Cataloging in Publication Data available

ISBN 978-1-4930-1564-1 (paperback)
ISBN 978-1-4930-1565-8 (e-book)

∞ ™ The paper used in this publication meets the minimum requirements
of American National Standard for Information Sciences—Permanence
of Paper for Printed Library Materials, ANSI/NISO Z39.48-1992.

CONTENTS

INTRODUCTION

WELCOME to all the information you need to know to Survive Mountains!

Knowing basic survival skills is critical to feeling comfortable and confident in the outdoors, no matter if you are heading out backpacking, snowmobiling through the backcountry, or even just driving on a remote dirt road through the mountains. The serenity and enjoyment of being in nature can quickly change into fear. Mother Nature can be very unforgiving, especially in the mountains. Storms, cold, steep terrain, whiteouts, swift rivers, and quickly changing weather are some of the threats. High elevations and mountainous terrain create additional challenges, but they can also create opportunities for shelter and safety if you know what to look for.

Knowing when and where to turn back is just as important as the skills to handle unforeseen circumstances. Sometimes unplanned situations are inevitable. Typically it will take multiple mistakes in sequence to compound a situation into a dangerous survival scenario. With the proper thought process and a correct decision, these can often be nipped in the bud and sent back on the right track. This book will explain the skills you will need to cope with these worst-case scenarios in mountainous environments.

The size and structure of the book is intended for quick reference, easy reading, and the ability to be tossed into your car or backpack with minimal encumbrance.

This entire book is streamlined and filled with how-tos, tips, and skills specifically focused on survival in the mountains. Initially it covers the essential survival kit and how to supplement if you are caught without any of these items. From there we move on to detail basic first aid and then a variety of survival shelters for various seasons and locations and how to stay warm and dry, including building a fire. The next step in your safety would be to find water and food. These will both be described in detail, including what to look for and what to avoid. Ultimately the book will conclude with orienteering, navigation, signaling tactics, and how to get located.

The most critical aspect of a survival situation is keeping a clear head and not panicking. This may seem trite, but it is 100 percent true. If you are in the moment without being terror-stricken, you will be able to think on your feet and adapt to the situation. In fact, that is part of the fun of an unexpected situation. Rely on your education and experience to be prudent and resourceful. Be confident and level-headed, and most importantly, optimistic. This book will prepare you for the worst and is written assuming that you have no equipment with you except the clothes on your back. Clearly this is not normally the situation if one is stuck in their car or lost while backpacking. The accessible gear should only make your survival situation easier and can easily be substituted in to make each step faster and more straightforward.

My goal is to get people outside. We need to reconnect with wilderness and value the remote places that we have left. I want you to have fun and experience the backcountry safely so that you aren't too intimidated to head out. Hopefully this book will help you accomplish that. It is streamlined so you can carry it to read in the backcountry, and even bring it along to try out the skills. Get comfortable with the techniques and the thought processes throughout the book and the situations will become second nature—in case the scenario really happens.

Jim "TRAUMA"

P.S. Remember to pack it in, pack it out; tread lightly; take only pictures, and leave only footprints; and practice Leave No Trace outdoors ethics—unless you are actually in a real survival situation and trying to signal for help. Visit LNT.org for more info.

THE BASICS

Your best chance of survival comes from simply staying calm, remaining positive, and keeping your thought process clear. If you get too stressed and worked up, your decision-making process will not be ideal. There is no definitive checklist for a survival situation because conditions change and potential injuries may come into play. It is important to have mental clarity in order to be adaptable to the situation. Remember to STOP—stop, think, observe, plan.

Another good acronym on how to handle an emergency situation is from the *US Army Survival Manual*: SURVIVAL.

S—size up the situation, including your surroundings, physical conditions, and equipment.

U—undo haste makes waste; use all of your senses.

R—remember where you are and the details of the route you decide to take.

V—vanquish fear and panic.

I—improvise and adapt tools and equipment for new purposes.

V—value living and never give up.

A—act like the natives and figure out how they survive.

L—live by your wits, but for now learn basic skills.

Most survival experts say that your best chance of rescue will occur within the first 72 hours of the missing person's report and the beginning of the search and rescue (SAR). This is often true, but SARs can be drawn out in mountainous regions because of bad weather conditions, and as a result it is essential to know how to maintain your safety for a few extra days. The easiest method to guarantee that a search will be started in a timely and efficient manner is to leave a detailed plan of your route and itinerary with somebody. Make sure to note the intended return time and then call that individual immediately when you exit the wilderness safely. This will ensure that you have a backup system in place, and SAR will be notified quickly and have a strategy of potential search locations.

If a survival situation ensues, most people say the motto is "Stay calm, stay put, and stay cool or stay warm (depending on the weather conditions)." This is generally true; however, certain situations dictate action. Remaining in the same place increases your chances of being found, gives you additional time to set up or build the necessary shelter and food-acquiring systems, and reduces the need for additional calorie intake compared to continued exertion. However, if you expect rescue to be delayed or not happen anytime soon, you should try to get out on your own. Travel safely and make sure to leave strong and obvious clues of your presence at the initial location and along the route you choose. If someone is seriously injured, a member of the group should go for help. Also if the location is not a good spot—for example, it is dangerous because of avalanche potential, water is located far away, or it is exposed to strong winds, cold, or thunderstorms—then move to a better location.

A tool that can easily remedy any potentially dangerous situation is a two-way communicator or personal locator beacon (PLB), like a DeLorme inReach or SPOT. A satellite phone can also work well but can be cost-prohibitive. Generally these devices can provide a quick way to send an SOS message embedded with your GPS coordinates. With these devices SAR will at least be activated immediately and instantly know your location. They may or may not be able to retrieve you quickly based on your location and the weather, but you will be guaranteed of their knowledge of the emergency and in a more timely fashion. Furthermore, with a two-way communicator you will be able to text message and communicate with the SAR incident commander in case you need to move locations or decide to keep moving toward civilization on your own.

These systems are better than relying on a cell phone in backcountry terrain. In most remote locations a cell phone will not have reception to send a message or call. However, if you do not have a PLB or two-way locator, keep in mind that even if you can't get a call or text out, your cell phone may be able to ping a nearby tower to provide an idea of your location. Be mindful of your battery power, though, as you don't want to run out of juice, and your battery will drain more rapidly in cold weather. In cold weather you may want to keep any electronics in an inside pocket of your jacket. Also, even if you are using these systems and have shared your GPS location, make sure to use signals and leave clues to speed up the search.

THE SURVIVAL KIT

The basics of the survival kit include:

- knife

- compass

- maps

- fire-starting tool

- fishing and/or hunting gear

- shelter

- signals

- medical supplies or first-aid kit

- water treatment

- insect protection

- emergency blanket

- cordage

- flashlight or headlamp

If you happen to have any of these with you, you are ahead of the game. You can get by without having any of these items, and that's what we'll describe in this section. We'll assume you are empty-handed as we go through how to get resourceful and create something from nothing.

KNIFE

A sharp object or knife is an integral piece of equipment and often the foundation for completing any of the subsequent necessary steps for survival that we will cover in detail in later chapters. Generally a sharp, jagged, or pointy rock or a sharp broken tree branch can suffice for most things that a knife will do. It won't cut quite as smoothly as a machine-made knife, but for the basics of cutting willows to make rope or slicing fish skin, you should be fine. Remember throughout your search for a knife that one implement may not be the best to perform all of the tasks, depending on the shape, size, and sharpness. Look near creeks and rivers for exposed rocks and branches, as this is often where you will find the largest selection and variety.

When you find a good shard to use as a knife, you can fairly easily turn it into a useful implement. Find a green piece of wood or a dry piece that is sturdy. Look for something about 6 to 10 inches long. Make sure it is still green so it isn't brittle. Using the shard, split one side in half about a third of the way down. Insert the shard with the pointed end protruding out. Then wrap some twine, hemp, or whatever cordlike material you have below the rock, then around the back of the rock to hold it in place, then finish and fasten the wrap above the rock. This will create a fairly sturdy hatchet to aid in most of the necessary survival steps you will have to perform. Keep in mind this isn't bombproof like a manufactured knife would be, but it will work well for skinning and gutting fish, creating kindling, and cutting small pieces of wood.

COMPASS

If you don't have a compass, don't fret. There are countless systems that we'll cover in the "Orienteering, Navigation, and Signaling" chapter to steer you in the right direction. The simplest methods need nothing more than observing the sun or the stars, or a wristwatch or a broken stick. More to come on how to use these methods!

MAPS

Maps are an integral component to know exactly where you are. In most survival situations, however, the person does not have a map. These situations could easily have been remedied with a map; for example, Chris McCandless of *Into the Wild* fame.

There are complex stargazing tactics to pinpoint your location, but you'll still need a map. Even with a GPS, you'll likely still need one. Coordinates will just be a random set of numbers without a map to place them on. Nowadays if you gain a high ridgeline or peak, you may be able to see some sign of human life, whether it's a building, road, or light. If that fails or you have an idea of your whereabouts, you probably already have an inkling of surrounding communities or roads, although they may be far away. Use this knowledge to your advantage, as stated in the last "L" of the SURVIVAL moniker, and head in that direction—making sure to maintain that bearing and not getting off track even more so.

Ultimately, since this book is catered toward survival in the mountains, after you have surveyed the scene from a high point and assessed your route, it will almost always be better to head lower in elevation. The temperatures will warm drastically (typically 3 to 5 degrees Fahrenheit per 1,000 feet of elevation), the weather will typically improve, flowing water will likely become more frequent, and you have a better chance of coming across other people or villages.

FIRE-STARTING TOOL

The simplest answer to starting a fire lies in carrying matches, a lighter, flint, or fire-starting tool. This is often not the case, or your lighter or matches may have gotten wet. It's not the end of the world when this happens, but it will definitely take more time and energy to get a fire going. You will simply need to assess what resources you have available and possible tree varieties. We will go into more details later in the "Fire" chapter. You will be looking for soft, non-resinous wood like aspen, cedar, basswood, cottonwood, or dry yucca stalks. Although pine is soft, it is not going to work well due to the sap, which causes cooling. You will need a few good pieces of wood, so grab them for later if you see them.

FISHING AND/OR HUNTING GEAR

Fish are relatively easy to catch and provide good nutrition. They are best cooked shortly after catching them. Usually it is easier to catch fish than to trap a land animal. The advantage of trapping a land animal is that you can make the trap and then let it do its thing while you go do something else. We will discuss technique later in the book, but for both systems you will generally need some cord, twine, string, or dental floss. This can be a shoelace, or you can make the cord from willows or other plants. Then you will need some sort of hook, which can be a sharpened piece of wood, a small thin bone, or a turtle shell. Traps are a little more complicated but will also only need some cord and wood, twigs, or rocks.

Remember, under the Leave No Trace ethics, don't catch or kill anything that you don't intend to eat or use for your survival.

SHELTER

Finding or making a shelter is an opportunity to get creative. Often in the mountains there are rock outcroppings or boulders with a cavity underneath. These are perfect spots where you won't have to expend much energy to improve them, and they will help retain heat from a fire. Other opportunities are using downed trees or branches to make cover. There are all sorts of varieties of shelters depending on the season and the vegetation. We'll cover these more later, but don't expect a five-star resort when you build your own shelter from scratch. The goal is warm, safe, and dry. Keep in mind when you are in your shelter that you may not be visible, so make sure to leave signals and clues as to your location.

SIGNALS

Flares are obvious signals, but I don't know anybody that carries them in the backcountry. More likely and common signals are fires, mirrors, and even rocks or boughs placed strategically in an open area like a meadow. Typically you want your signal to be visible from high above. Size is very important because something that seems big to you on the ground may be hardly visible from thousands of feet above. Tree cover will severely limit the visibility, so meadows, ridgelines, and open hillsides may be your best bet. Build a large X with tree branches and rocks that will stand out. If you can find them, red rocks, or rocks that are a different color than the ground, would be very helpful.

MEDICAL SUPPLIES

A typical first-aid kit contains pain killers and anti-inflammatory medicine, bandages, gauze, antiseptic, tape, soap or gloves for hygiene, needle and thread, prescription medicine if needed, scissors, foot and blister care products, and maybe even Benadryl. These items can be handy, but to be honest, most of these supplies are superfluous and can easily be replaced by ingenuity. Techniques will be discussed in detail in the "Basic First Aid" chapter.

WATER TREATMENT

Generally all backcountry water sources should be treated. Treatments include iodine, UV light, chlorine dioxide, or boiling or filtering the water. Even if treating the water, try to gather it from streams or other moving water. It tastes better and is usually safer.

INSECT PROTECTION

In mountainous areas insects can be swarming in the springtime. After the winter thaws and when the temperatures have warmed sufficiently, they can be bloodthirsty. Typically there are not many diseases born from insects in high mountain locales, and they will be more of a nuisance than a threat. That having been said, they can be a severe nuisance. Without any human-made repellants at

Insects can be a big nuisance in the mountains during certain seasons. In this location this was five minutes worth of swatting mosquitoes.

hand, the best way to avoid insect bites is to either add clothing that they can't bite through, like nylon wind shells or rain jackets, if you have them, or slather yourself in mud. Cake the mud on and let it dry. Insects shouldn't be able to penetrate through it. Repeat as necessary. Sometimes in the mountains, if you are lucky, you may be able to find cedars, onions, or mints and use the plant oils as insect repellant.

EMERGENCY BLANKET

A standard lightweight Mylar space blanket is an easy layer to throw on for increased warmth. It does a fantastic job of reflecting your body heat back on you, or casting the heat from fire to where you want it so it isn't lost. These blankets are pocket-size and usually weigh less than a few ounces.

CORDAGE

Carrying some parachute cord or twine will save you a lot of time if you end up getting into a survival situation. It is possible to make your own from plants or materials that you can find, but the time involved is considerable and the end quality is likely to be marginal at best. As a result it can be beneficial to carry a minimum of a few feet of cordage.

FLASHLIGHT OR HEADLAMP

A flashlight or headlamp is not a must-have but obviously a very helpful piece of equipment to work or continue moving at night. A headlamp is highly recommended over a flashlight since you can work with both hands at the same time and the light beam will follow the movement of your head and thus your field of view. Generally you will also get more efficiency in weight and function from a head-lamp rather than a flashlight.

BASIC FIRST AID

Sometimes a survival situation arises because of an injury. It is imperative to know how to handle these situations calmly, correctly, and efficiently, while still only requiring minimal supplies and resources. This guide isn't meant to be all-inclusive but should cover most emergency injuries.

BASICS

First step is scene safety. If you or the patient will be in danger of getting injured, or injured worse, you either shouldn't approach the scene or should move the patient out of the dangerous area. Then try to keep as clean and sterile of a situation as possible, even if it is just washing your hand in a creek quickly before and after. Ultimately the most important thing is ABCC—in that order.

- **A**—Airway
- **B**—Breathing
- **C**—Circulation
- **C**—C-Spine

If somebody is seriously injured, the first step is activating your PLB or emergency beacon, if you have one, or sending someone for help. Then you want to make sure the patient's airway is functioning, otherwise they won't be able to get air in or out. Look in their mouth and thrust their jaw forward, without jostling the neck, to try to open the airway. Hopefully they will be able to exchange air and be breathing normally. If they are not breathing, start rescue breathing (mouth to mouth) and check their pulse every couple of minutes.

For C, you want to make sure there isn't any major bleeding that would cause the patient to bleed out. If there is, take care of it through elevation, compression, and bandaging. If nothing is stopping the bleeding, start a tourniquet and make sure to write the time of application on the limb. C also includes circulation, as in making sure the heart is beating and perfusing the body. If the heart is not beating, chest compressions must begin and should be performed firmly and at a rate of 100 per minute along the breastbone just above the nipple line. Be prepared that if you are doing it correctly and firmly enough, you will probably break some ribs.

Finally, the last C stands for c-spine, which means cervical spine. These are the top seven vertebrae in the spinal column from the base of the brain through the neck to the bony protrusion at the base of the neck. These are the most susceptible to a life-threatening injury since if someone breaks the top two or three vertebrae they can immediately stop breathing. If there is a displaced fracture it can move and sever the spinal cord. If a c-spine injury is suspected, try not to move the patient and brace his or her head and neck with your hands, arms, or knees to try to prevent any movement at all.

EXTREMITY INJURIES

Extremity injuries are generally closed injuries and can usually be taken care of by splinting. If the patient is bleeding, make sure to stop the bleeding by applying a bandage and elevating the injury. A bandage can be as simple as wrapping strips of material, like someone's shirt, around the injury. After controlling the bleeding, splint the injury to prevent movement. This requires splinting the joint above and below the injury if it is a long bone, or the bone above and below if it is a joint. Use materials that you have or can find to perform these functions. It can be sticks, pieces of driftwood, tape, trekking poles, and willows to secure the system.

If the fracture is open and bleeding, or if there is a loss of feeling, numbness, or tingling distal to the injury, you want to gently realign the injury into anatomical position before securing a splint to the injured area.

HEAD INJURIES

Head injuries can present in many different ways and can be very deceptive. It is important to monitor a person with a head injury accordingly. They may have minimal symptoms initially but can later present with a screaming headache, nausea, dizziness, vomiting, and some serious side effects that can come on hours after the event. These situations are very serious, and a rapid rescue from the backcountry is imperative.

Generally treat a head injury as you would most other injuries. Stop the bleeding, bandage to keep it clean, and compress the area, and monitor the situation to make sure things don't deteriorate. Head injuries can be scary because they can include dizziness, repetition in speech, combative behavior, and almost drunk-like symptoms. Most symptoms will improve with time, but if things start to get worse, the situation has escalated and the injured party needs to get out of the backcountry as fast as possible.

+Tip: Willow bark has a similar active ingredient as aspirin. In fact, that's where aspirin derived from. If you are not allergic to aspirin and have an injury, muscle pain, or fever in the backcountry, break off a piece of willow and chew the bark to release the salicin, or you can make a tea by steeping the bark in hot water.

COLD INJURIES

Depending on the season, temperatures in the mountains can get bitterly cold. Be prepared for cold injuries in this environment, especially if you are dealing with travel through snow continually. It is imperative to make sure that your extremities and core are warm.

Hypothermia

Snow will quickly melt into your clothing and zap your body heat without the proper layers. Be aware of the possibility of hypothermia. Dehydration and lack of food will also increase your chances of hypothermia.

To treat hypothermia, it is imperative to warm the body. The first step is typically to add layers or strip off the wet layers of clothing. Replace lost fluids and eat to maintain calories that will help warm the body.

Hypothermia can result in sluggish thinking, poor decision-making, loss of dexterity, and an unexplained feeling of warmth. Ultimately it will also lead to an inability to take care of one's self, unconsciousness, and death.

It is crucial to rewarm a hypothermia patient as soon as you see the early stages. This can be done by body-to-body contact inside a sleeping bag or near a fire. Make sure to remove any wet clothing. In a serious case of hypothermia, take care not to rewarm the body too rapidly. Also once rewarmed, make sure not to let the body get cold again once removed from the heat source.

Frostbite

Frostbite is the result of frozen tissue. Frostnip is the first step as the skin gets cold and loses circulation. You may feel numbness or tingling before you lose feeling in the area. The longer it is exposed to the cold, the deeper the injured tissue will be and the more serious the injury. Be aware of the sensation in your face, feet, ears, and hands, as these are the most susceptible areas. Skin will look dull, whitish, and pale.

If you are with someone, they can monitor your face for the signs. If you are alone, you need to be aware of the loss of sensation to any of these areas. You can also periodically cover your nose and cheeks with a gloved hand to provide some warmth to the skin. If your hands are cold,

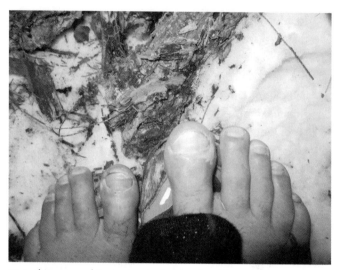
Note the waxy white texture indicating frostbite and tissue damage.

place them in your armpits or groin to keep them warmer. Also make sure to scrunch and make faces and move your fingers and toes from time to time to increase the blood flow. If you lose feeling in your hands or feet, stop to assess the damage. If it doesn't seem deep, rewarm the affected areas by using body heat or placing the injuries next to a

+Tip: If you have or find ziplock bags, bread bags, or other plastic bags, these can be put over your socks or hands to create a vapor barrier liner and increase the warmth for your extremities by not permitting air exchange.

Get creative! In this case plastic bags give added warmth and moisture protection.

hot water bottle. Do not insert the frostbite into hot or warm water. You want to rewarm the injured areas slowly.

Most importantly, if you don't believe you have the proper equipment to keep the area from refreezing, refrain from thawing the injured tissue. It will do more damage to thaw the area and have it refreeze and raise the chance of infection. Always avoid massaging areas with frostbite to rewarm them.

SNOW BLINDNESS

Bright sunlight in a snow-covered area can cause snow blindness. It happens when ultraviolet light damages the cornea. Initial symptoms include a feeling of grit in the

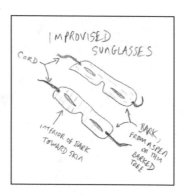

IMPROVISED SUNGLASSES

CORD

INTERIOR OF BARK TOWARD SKIN

BARK FROM ASPEN OR THIN BARKED TREE

eyes, pain in and around the eyes that often increases with movement of the eyeball, teary and red eyes, and a headache that usually increases with continued light exposure. Additional exposure can cause permanent eye damage.

To prevent the condition, wear sunglasses or make a makeshift pair from tree bark, thin wood, or cardboard. You can also rub ash underneath your eyes to reduce the glare, as baseball players do with the eye black. To treat snow blindness, you will need to bandage your eyes and prevent exposure to light until the symptoms go away.

HEAT INJURIES

Mountainous regions are typically cool in temperature, but there is still the possibility of heat-related injuries.

Heat cramps are caused by the loss of salt from excessive sweating. Typically the cramps will be in the arms, legs, or abdomen. They will start as mild cramps but can gain in intensity. You should stop activity and take a break in the shade if the cramps begin. Make sure to drink plenty of water.

Heat exhaustion is caused by fluid loss and salt or electrolyte loss. Symptoms include headache, dizziness, mental confusion, irritability, excessive sweating, weakness, and pale, moist, clammy skin. If this occurs, immediately seek shade and water and rest out of the sun. Sprinkle the patient with water every few minutes and have them drink a small amount of water every 3 to 5 minutes.

Heat stroke is the more serious form caused by extreme lack of water and salts and the body's subsequent inability to cool itself. This is a serious condition and could lead to death if the patient is not cooled immediately. Symptoms include nausea and vomiting, mental confusion, unconsciousness, headache, dizziness, and most importantly, a lack of sweat and hot, dry skin because the body isn't functioning properly to cool itself. A person with heat stroke should be cooled by pouring water on them and fanning them.

ALTITUDE SICKNESS OR ACUTE MOUNTAIN SICKNESS (AMS)

In the mountains some people will feel the beginning stages of altitude sickness above 6,000 feet elevation. Above 9,000 feet, the symptoms can become more severe and require an immediate descent. The primary initial symptoms are headache, nausea, coughing, wheezing, difficulty breathing, and fatigue. Without descending to a lower elevation or giving your body a chance to acclimate, these symptoms can progress and become increasingly

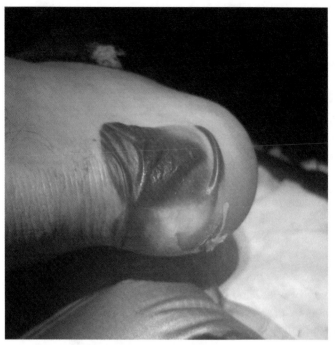

Blisters and rubbing can come on quickly from your shoes, especially when they are wet or sweaty.

serious, and even lead to life-threatening health issues like cerebral or pulmonary edema. Make sure to drink plenty of fluids and listen to your body. If you are not feeling well, descend to a lower elevation. It is important to drink lots of water, since cold air contains less moisture than warm air and your body will be losing additional water to the outside environment.

DEHYDRATION

Everybody knows what dehydration is. The simple solution is to drink more water. It is important to mention that in cold weather you may not think you are losing fluids, but you still are. You may not need as much water as in warm climates, but you still need to check the color of your urine. Cold weather typically increases urine output, but decreases body fluids that you have to replace. If your urine is dark yellow, you are becoming dehydrated and need to drink more water.

SUNBURN

The sun can be intense at high elevations. Snow can also exacerbate the sun's rays. Be aware that you can get sunburn even in below-freezing temperatures. The sun's rays can reflect in all directions off the snow and can burn the bottom of your nose, the roof of your mouth if your mouth is open, or the back of your knees. If sunburn will be an issue, you can cover your skin with mud and let it cake in place to resist the sun's rays.

SURVIVAL SHELTERS

The weather can get nasty in the mountains and exposure is a serious threat, especially in the winter. It is critical to make a good shelter in a protected location when the weather is not ideal. Often the temperatures drop significantly over-night in mountainous regions. Make sure to find a good, safe, and protected location. Stay away a little from bodies of water, meadows, and low depressions where cold air will settle at night. Often the temperature will be over 10 degrees colder in these places. Setting up shelter under a nice tree will help maintain a warmer temperature, since the tree will prevent the long-wave radiation from the earth from escaping into the night sky. Also be mindful of high ground, as the winds are usually stronger.

A solid shelter should be big enough to sleep com-fortably in, but not so big that you'll have to warm excess space. It is important to get decent sleep to maintain a high energy level, a clear head, and a positive outlook.

Deciding what type of shelter to set up requires evaluat-ing the terrain, weather, climate, and available resources. If something unexpected has happen like a car or plane crash, your best bet will usually be to use those materials to create a shelter, as long as it is safe from fire or leaking flammable fluids like gasoline.

A cold, windy, horrible spot to set up a shelter. Scout the surroundings and you can see by dropping not too far that you would find a much more protected camping location.

Also think about how much time investment you should put into constructing the shelter. If you only expect to be out a day before being rescued, why create a bombproof shelter? Likewise if you expect to try to walk out or seek a new location the next morning. Building a good shelter is a considerable time commitment, so you may be better off constructing a series of temporary shelters if you intend to walk out. Also keep in mind how much daylight you have left when deciding what type of shelter to construct, as the last thing you want is to leave the site to collect resources and be unable to find it again.

Now here's how to set up a shelter with only what you will find in the forest.

SUMMER

In the summer, even if the temperatures are warm, they can easily plummet in the mountains when inclement weather arrives. Hypothermia is common in the summer as well. The key to remaining warm is to stay dry. As a result, it is important to have a shelter in place in case the weather takes a turn for the worse.

If you have a poncho with you, you can easily make a poncho lean-to and it will be a simple solution. Make sure to face the back of the poncho into the wind as you choose a site to set up. You don't want the wind blowing into the raised side of the lean-to. To construct this shelter, find trees or a downed log. Attach cord to one side of the poncho and tie off to the trees or log. Stake or anchor the other side of the poncho into the ground. You will now have a relatively protected area underneath the poncho.

Lean-to set up.

To adjust the "living space" and headroom under the poncho, just raise or lower the attachments to the trees. You can also add a branch or stick in the middle to create a center support. Just make sure it isn't sharp and won't puncture your poncho.

You can also set up a poncho in an A-frame style by attaching the center to two trees and anchoring the corners. This provides better coverage in storms.

The easiest way to "build" a good, weatherproof shelter if you don't have a tarp or poncho is to find a rock alcove or cave. Another way is to pile rocks to construct a barrier on the windward side to prevent the wind from blowing in. If precipitation is imminent, you can also add additional walls and drape pine boughs or other sticks and

A-frame style set up.

broad-leafed foliage across the top to block the rain or snow. You can also look for downed trees to use as the support for the roof and pile sticks and foliage to make an A-frame-style structure or a lean-to.

It will save a lot of time when building if you can find a good log or start for the shelter, a relatively flat foundation, and an area with an abundance of good materials. Try to locate your shelter fairly close to a water source, near the materials that you will need to build it, and near an open area. You want to be safe from the elements and exposure but don't want to hide your location so well that you would be overlooked by a search party or aerial search. Make sure to leave signs and signals outside your shelter and in the open area.

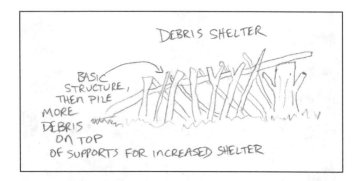

To build a debris shelter from tree branches, start by creating a tripod with two short branches and a long branch from the ridgeline. You can also raise the end of the branch away from the tripod to create a longer elevated area inside. Pile branches and limbs against the ridgepole, ensuring that it is stable, creates enough space on the inside for your body, and is steep enough to shed rain. Add other finer debris in the opposite direction. Then pile grass, pine needles, and leaves all over the top. The thicker the better, as this will also create insulation to keep your body heat inside the shelter. Finally add more sticks and branches over the debris to keep the smaller debris in place if it is stormy.

WINTER

In the winter you can look for the same opportunities that may arise by using a natural shelter, but you can also make one using the snow. Snow is a very good insulator. This can be an advantage to help keep the temperature just below freezing inside your shelter so it won't plunge into the single digits or even below zero.

You can make a snow cave, igloo, trench, or quinzhee. Each is a great option for winter camping; however, they can be time-consuming to make. If you're building it by yourself, allot about 2 to 3 hours. A trench is the fastest system to build. An igloo is the most time-consuming and not the best method for lightweight hiking and backpacking; it can require a snow saw and takes a lot of work to pack the snow. A quinzhee, or quinzee, is basically a snow cave, except you pile snow into a dome to make the cave because there isn't enough snow to dig a cave out. If you're making a quinzhee, make sure the snow settles enough to bond together. This can take a few hours, so you'll need to check it over time. Without proper snow consolidation, the roof may collapse.

Snow caves require a lot of snow and a spot that's out of avalanche danger. In order to find a spot safe from avalanches, look for a slope that is gentler than 30 degrees. Also take caution of being below steep slopes, even if the terrain is mellow where you are, and below cornices.

Look for a snow bank or drift to build a snow cave in. Start by digging a tunnel for the cave. The tunnel should be wider than your shoulders and should slope up toward the cave. That way cold air will settle outside the cave opening. Hollow out a cavity in the snow for the cave. Make it

+Tip: If new batteries aren't working in winter, it's most likely because they're cold. Warm them up in an inside pocket or close to your skin. You may also want to carry them in your pocket for a while when you know you are going to use your electronics.

+Tip: Keep in mind that you will lose as much as 80 percent of your body heat to the ground when you are sleeping. Use an insulating material like leaves or pine boughs to reduce this heat loss and sleep better.

tall enough to sit upright in and big enough for you and your companions to lie down. Pack the roof of the cave, and smooth the surface so that it doesn't drip on you or your gear.

If you have space in the cave, you can make benches out of the snow, keeping you off the ground and above some of the cold air. Poke a trekking pole, ski pole, tree branch, or avalanche probe through the ceiling of the cave for ventilation. Cover the floor or the benches with waterproof material. Put your backpack in the doorway to block cold air and keep the cave warmer.

Snow trenches are the easiest and fastest winter shelters to make, but they're not as comfortable or as warm as a snow cave. Also, they're not recommended if you're expecting a lot of snow, because they don't have strong roofs. Dig a trench at least 3 feet deep, 6 feet long, and 3 to 4 feet wide for each person, with an entrance at one end. Lay your poles, skis, or smooth tree branches across the width of the trench. Spread your tarp, rain fly, or emergency blanket over the trench. Anchor the sides by covering the edges with snow, tree branches, or rocks.

DRYING AND PREVENTING GEAR FROM FREEZING IN COLD CONDITIONS

Eventually your winter gear is likely to get wet, whether it's your shoes from hiking through snow all day or your gloves, socks, or other layers of gear. Wet or moist clothing leads to losing body heat and the potential for hypothermia and frostbite.

Since winter temperatures usually don't get above freezing in the mountains, the only way to dry gloves and clothes is to wear them, hang them in your shelter, or sleep with them in your sleeping bag. When I have moist—not soaked—clothes at the end of the day, I prefer keeping them with me in my sleeping bag. I'll either wear them to bed underneath dry layers or put them in dead space within the sleeping bag.

Frozen footwear is painful to put on and wear. To keep your boots, shoes, or boot liners from freezing overnight, sleep with them in your sleep system or sleeping bag's foot box, or a dead space in your sleeping bag. If your boots are wet, put them in a waterproof bag, in a pack liner or stuff sack, before putting them in your sleeping bag. Shake any dirt, mud, or excess snow off before putting them in your sleeping bag or in a stuff sack. Turn your pack liner inside out so that when you pack up the next day, you are placing your gear into the dry side of the pack liner.

FIRE

If you are carrying a lighter or matches, it is crucial to pack it well so it won't get wet. That will help bypass some of the next steps, which can be time-consuming and unnerving. If I am cold and wet, I want to know that I will be able to start a fire on a dime. Being comfortable making a fire can get you out of trouble and is one of your last lines of defense against the elements. The warmth of a fire can be the difference between life and death.

It can take a lot of effort and calories to even get close to the point where you are able to start a fire, without having any modern-day tools to aid the process. Making fire without a lighter or matches takes practice and should be nailed down before any life-threatening situation actually

+Tip: It's much easier to keep a fire active than to restart it, so try to keep it going once you have started it. If you need to leave your shelter site for a long time, you can put hardwood on the fire, which will take longer to burn. Another option is while the coals are still fairly large, gather them into a pile so they will burn slower or put on a larger log that will take a while to burn through. Keep in mind that limiting the available air by putting the fuel closer together will also slow the burning process.

happens. Plus, it is fun and empowering to make a fire the old-fashioned way.

I have included descriptions of a bow-drill set and the fire plow technique. If you need to choose between the two, I recommend the bow-drill set. Both methods require energy, persistence, and practice; however, the bow adds mechanical advantage to the system and helps create additional friction.

BOW-DRILL SET

This is the easiest way to get a coal going so you will be able to start a fire, though it takes time to build. I have built bow-drill sets on occasion for fun and to kill time. However, it only makes sense if your matches or lighter have stopped working and you are in an emergency situation where you are stationary and waiting for help. Otherwise, it is too time-consuming, and you'll likely be traveling to seek help or an exit out of the backcountry.

- Equipment needed: knife, wood from forest, parachute cord or buckskin or moistened rawhide

- Drill: best with cottonwood, birch, alder, sycamore, and willow

- Fire board: best with cottonwood or dead willow

- Tinder: inner bark of cottonwood or dry flammable material like shredded tree bark, bird's nest, or leaves

- Handhold: a wood harder than the drill, like juniper or oak, or you can use antler or bone

+Tip: If you would like to bring a coal with you because you are traveling to a new site, you can surround a large coal with smaller coals and tinder and create a protective shell using rocks or bark to carry the coal. It should remain active for several hours if the weather is decent and it isn't too cold. Depending on your location, you can also use the female flower head of the cattail, the true tinder fungus, or false tinder fungus as slow matches that will burn for a couple of hours.

Here are the basics of how to make this primitive fire starter:

Socket: Should be an easily gripped piece of hardwood, rock, or bone with a depression in one side. It is used to hold the drill in place and put downward pressure onto the drill.

Drill: A straight piece of seasoned hardwood about 2 centimeters in diameter and 25 centimeters long. The top end is pointed and the bottom end is blunt in order to focus the friction onto the fire board.

Fire board: Can vary in size based on available wood. Shoot for 2.5 centimeters thick and 10 centimeters wide. It could be a seasoned softwood or of the same material as the drill. Cut a depression about 2 centimeters from the edge on one of the long sides of the board. On the underside, opposite the depression, cut a V-shaped notch from the edge of the board to the depression. This will help channel the punk (hot black powder) into a pile and create a coal. You can put a leaf or piece of paper underneath the notch to help transfer the coal to your tinder.

Bow: The bow should be made of a tough green stick. This will help it last longer and hold up to abuse. Look for one about 2.5 centimeters in diameter. It can be made of any resilient type of wood. The bowstring can be any type of cord. Tie the bowstring from one end of the bow to the other, with minimal slack. When you wrap the drill into the bow string, you want it to be tight, but if the bow string is tied too tight, it will be difficult to loop the drill into the system.

Step 1: Place some dry tinder, a leaf, or paper underneath the notch in the fire board.

Step 2: Place one foot on the fire board. Loop the bowstring over the drill, and place the drill in the depression on the fire board.

+Tip: If you are getting cold, you have a few options to stay warm: (1) Keep moving/hiking. (2) Do jumping jacks to get your blood moving. (3) Make a fire. (4) Eat something with a high calorie content; your body needs calories to stay warm. On cold, rainy days, it is tempting to push through without stopping. Your body needs to refuel. Keep snacks and a lunch handy so that you can take quick breaks or eat while you are walking.

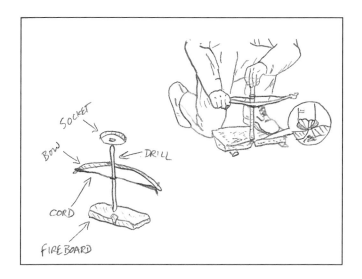

Step 3: Place the socket in your other hand on top of the drill to hold it in position.

Step 4: Press down on the drill and move the bow back and forth, spinning the drill.

Step 5: Once you have the routine and a smooth motion, increase the downward pressure and the speed of the bow. It can help to place the wrist of the hand that is holding the socket directly against the shin of your leg that is stepping on the fire board. This will add stability to the system as you increase the pace. The resulting increase in friction will cause punk to carry into the notch. Enough punk will result in a coal.

Step 6: When you get a coal, or a glowing ember, collect the punk and place it in the "nest" of tinder. Blow on the tinder until it ignites.

If you don't have any cordage, you might have to use the hand-drill or fire plow technique to start a fire. It is a bit harder, as there is no mechanical advantage. The hand-drill technique is the same as the bow-drill but instead of using the bow to create the mechanical advantage, you are rubbing your hands together around the spindle to create the movement. The same principles apply, as friction and speed are going to create the coal.

FIRE PLOW TECHNIQUE

Following is how you would get the fire plow going:

Step 1: Use the same type of wood as mentioned in the bow-drill set, but you should make your fire board a bit wider.

Step 2: Cut a small channel down the middle of the fire board, extending all the way to the end of the board.

Step 3: Place some dry grass or tinder below the end of the fire board.

Step 4: Start running the drill down the channel on the fire board. Once you have the routine, increase speed and pressure only pushing in the downward

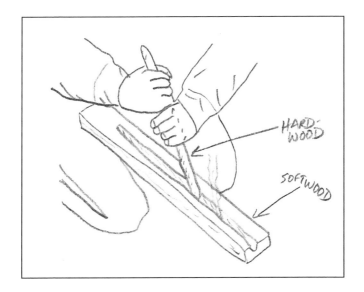

direction on the fire board. The resulting increase in friction will cause punk to carry into the notch at the bottom. Enough punk will result in a coal.

Step 5: When you get a coal, or a glowing ember, collect the punk and place it in a "nest" of tinder. Blow on the tinder until it ignites.

Once you get your tinder to catch, you will then have to increasingly add sticks and twigs of larger diameter. It can be difficult to get these to catch, and it is important to have this set up beforehand and have some good, dry tinder ready. The tepee or log cabin method to get the fire rolling works well. Here's how . . .

HOW TO BUILD A FIRE

Fires are the essence of camping and a key tool for survival, but under normal circumstances, I never build them. I can count on one hand all the times I have built a campfire. The majority of those times, the campfire was a miniscule twig smudge to create smoke to keep the mosquitoes at bay.

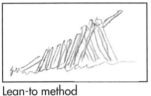

Lean-to method

Tepee method

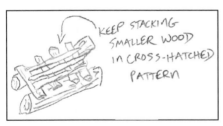

KEEP STACKING SMALLER WOOD IN CROSS-HATCHED PATTERN

Pyramid method

HOW TO BUILD A FIRE WITH WET WOOD

Step 1: Accumulate some small pieces of wood, twigs, or dry leaves to get started. This may entail searching under trees, digging into lower layers of

+Tip: If you have some dry cotton material, like a bandanna, you can make a char cloth to help you start a fire. Turn your stove on and place 2-by-2-inch squares of cotton in your pot and cover it. In a few minutes you should start to see a decent amount of smoke. When the smoke stops, shut off your stove and let it cool down. You should have charred squares of fabric that will easily catch a spark and burn slowly. When you blow on the char cloth, it should help your tinder burn. You can also use any petroleum-based product, such as ChapStick, DEET, or Vaseline, or your toilet paper stash to help get your fire started.

the duff, or using an inner layer of tree bark. Depending on your location, the optimal fuel sources for starting a fire will vary, but always try to find dry, downed wood.

Step 2: Make a tepee with small sticks, and put some twigs and dry debris in the middle. Light the debris and small sticks using your lighter. If necessary, pour a little bit of your stove fuel onto the debris and sticks. You can also soak a stick or dip it into your fuel bottle before adding it to the fire. Don't go too heavy with the stove fuel; you don't want to use it all on the first try. You might need to add some more fuel if the first attempt doesn't work.

Step 3: If the fire catches, let the sticks burn a bit and create some coals before you start adding more wood and slightly larger pieces. Build up the size of the additional wood so that you don't smother your fire. If need be, add a little more stove fuel to get things going. White gas is very volatile; it flares up and quickly dies down. Alcohol burns for a longer time but at a lower temperature. Both can be beneficial. Fire travels upwards, so it can help to put the fuel below things that you are attempting to make catch.

Step 4: If your fire still isn't lighting, remember to start small. Use small pieces of dry tinder. It can also be helpful to use your knife and strip off the wet outsides of the pieces of wood you are using. Try to get down to dry areas, and keep your fuel in a dry place. An abandoned bird's nest can make great tinder, as can dead lower limbs on evergreen trees. In western forests, some coniferous trees accumulate large amounts of sap on the outside of the bark. Tree sap can also help you get your fire started. It catches easily and burns well.

If the fire isn't starting no matter what you do, you need to set up your shelter and put on dry clothes or head for the car or for civilization, depending on the time of day. Know when to cut your losses and keep moving to stay warm. You need to prevent hypothermia, and moving will keep you warm. Plan to head lower in elevation, and hopefully the bad weather will pass quickly. For now you must think about your immediate well-being. Keep moving and eat

+Tip: To build a fire on snow-covered ground, you need to create a platform of wet wood on top of the snow. Make a solid platform using wet or rotten wood in one direction and then cross-hatch it in the opposite direction. This will prevent the snow from melting underneath your fire and wetting the wood and coals. Using moist wood will prevent it from burning out rapidly or catching fire.

WOOD PLATFORM FOR FIRE IN SNOW-COVERED AREA

occasionally, even if you are not feeling hungry. Make sure to reference the map or your navigation strategies to keep on target as you head for civilization.

WATER

Water is one of the main ingredients for survival, since you will only be able to survive a few days without having any and you will quickly become dehydrated, which can lead to headaches, fatigue, dizziness, fainting, and nonsensical thought patterns. This can ultimately spiral the situation that you are already in, but at least it is usually easier to find water in mountain environments. You may have snow to melt, running water coming from glacial melt, or copious amounts of running water or lakes. Often the topography and surrounding vegetation can give telltale signs of where you will find water. The presence of willows, alders, and dense, green, brushy creek beds can be signs of running water.

Generally you should plan on treating the water that you find in the backcountry, but if you don't have that option, do what you need to do to survive. If you can't treat the water and can obtain it directly from snowmelt or a spring coming straight out of the ground, you will minimize your chance of illness. Try to obtain water from a running source over a stationary body of water to minimize your risk of waterborne illness. If you have a fire going, you can boil water to make it potable. Also, you can filter scuzzy water through your shirt or a bandanna to help remove the floating debris.

+Tip: Keep your water bottle from freezing by only filling it three-quarters of the way and placing it upside down in your pack's side pocket. This prevents water from freezing in the bottle's mouth—unless it's really cold out. In extreme cold, keep your water bottle in an insulated pouch. You can also warm or boil your water before putting it in your bottle or the pouch. A thermos will also work but weighs more.

Another great way to gather potable water is to catch rain if the weather is bad. Rainwater is safe and potable until it makes contact with the ground. You can gather rainwater by using large leaves or other impermeable surfaces and collecting or channeling the water into a pot, bowl-shaped rock, or other nonporous catchment system.

If you are having trouble finding water, you can use the following methods to get some, but it is much less efficient than finding a natural water source. The solar still will provide safe, potable drinking water.

SOLAR STILL FOR GETTING WATER

Equipment needed: plastic ground sheet or waterproof pack liner

Underground still: Dig a hole about 2 feet deep and line it with one or a half of your plastic pieces. Either pee into the plastic liner or add a bunch of green foliage into the hole. Put your pot in the center, lowest part of the hole, and on top of the liner. You can also throw some fresh foliage in there. Cover the hole with the other plastic piece, and place rocks around the border. Drop a small rock in

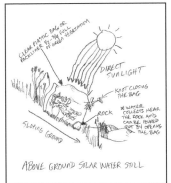

ABOVE GROUND SOLAR WATER STILL

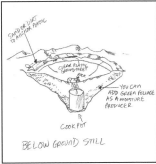

BELOW GROUND STILL

the middle right over your pot so that the water/pee will condense on the plastic and then drip down into the pot. This process can be used to get water and also to treat it.

Aboveground still: Put green foliage into your pack liner. Weigh one corner down with a rock, and tie the mouth of the bag closed above that. Place the bag in direct sunlight. Remove the water by untying the mouth of the bag and pouring out the water. Then reseal the bag to collect more.

CLOTH TECHNIQUE FOR GETTING WATER
Equipment needed: bandanna or base layer

You can collect condensation, dew, or steam from boiling water with your bandanna or base layer. Then you wring out the bandanna to provide water.

FOOD

Food is important in a survival situation but generally in mountain environments can fall behind water and shelter in importance. You can live for weeks without food or even longer while surviving on a reduced calorie diet. It is important to try to maintain calorie intake in order to keep your body functioning properly and your thought process clear. In addition, without proper calorie consumption, it is likely that you will have more trouble staying warm. In the mountains, which typically have storms or cold weather, this can easily complicate the situation even more.

A critical component to thinking about food in a survival scenario is to be able to step out of your comfort zone. Keep in mind that many insects are edible, including crickets, June bugs, lice, many species of ants, grasshoppers, dragonflies, and earthworms, to name a few. You can eat many insects raw or toast them over a fire, and they provide a fairly nutritious protein-filled food. Insects provide 65 to 80 percent protein, compared to 20 percent for beef. Avoid insects that sting or bite, are hairy or brightly colored, or have a pungent odor. Also stay away from spiders and insects that are known to carry diseases, like ticks, mosquitoes, and flies. When searching for insects, look under down trees, rotting logs, or in grassy areas. You can often find large concentrations of insects in these locations. Don't forget to look underground also if there is a path to an underground nest.

Larger animals will be much harder to catch and prepare, so typically they are not worth the effort. Concentrate on smaller animals, which are more abundant and easier to prepare. Most animals that crawl, swim, walk, or fly are edible.

It doesn't make sense to hunt for game unless you are going to be stationary for a couple of days. You are better off moving toward your next resupply and looking for edible plants, which are more common and require less time and energy to acquire. Make sure to eat only plants and mushrooms that you can positively identify. I recommend steering clear of mushrooms in an emergency situation. Identifying mushrooms can be difficult and must be precise. Many species look similar and there is not much room for experimentation, since some mushrooms are highly toxic even in low doses.

If you get into a tough situation and run out of food, here are some general guidelines to follow on recognizing edible plants without carrying a guidebook.

GENERAL RULES FOR EDIBLE PLANTS
Generally speaking, "Leaves of three, let them be. Leaves of four, eat some more."

Other general rules to avoid potentially harmful plants are to stay away from any wild or unknown plants that have:

- Milky or discolored sap

+Tip: Lichens exist in most alpine environments. There are no poisonous lichens. You can soak them overnight and then boil them in water to remove the acids and the disagreeable taste.

- Beans, bulbs, or seeds inside a pod

- Three-leaved growth pattern

- Grain heads with black, purple, or pink spurs

- Almond scent in woody parts and leaves

- Dill-, carrot-, parsnip-, or parsley-like foliage

- Spines, hairs, or thorns

- Bitter or soapy taste

Note legumes in the foreground. Most legumes are not edible.

+Tip: Most new growth on coniferous trees is edible and rich in vitamins. You will see it is a brighter green on the ends of the boughs. You can either eat this or steep it to make a nutritious tea. Just stay clear from eating anything from cedar trees since they are poisonous.

If you are trying a new plant or berry, ingest small quantities. Allow at least 24 hours before eating more. If you are trying to identify potential edible plants, do not ingest more than one unknown plant in a 24-hour period. If you can safely ingest the plant, make sure the plant is abundant enough to be worth your while. Keep in mind that some plants have parts that are edible and other parts that are not.

HOW TO IDENTIFY POISONOUS PLANTS AND TREAT REACTIONS

Poison ivy, poison oak, poison sumac, and stinging nettle are fairly common on parts of the Appalachian Trail (AT) and Pacific Coast Trail (PCT), and on lots of other hiking trails in the United States. Know what they look like, and do your best to avoid them.

Poison sumac and stinging nettle are a little harder to discern than poison ivy and poison oak, but they are respectively less common and less irritating. Stinging nettles only usually burn for about 15 minutes and don't leave a residual rash, so they are relatively harmless. If you rinse and then cook or boil stinging nettles, they are edible and nutritious. They taste like cooked spinach.

Identification

"Leaves of three, let them be" is a good rule of thumb for both poison ivy and poison oak.

Poison ivy: Three pointed leaflets with smoothed or toothed edges and varying in length from 2 to 4 inches. It can grow as ground cover, a shrub, or a vine. The leaves are often reddish in spring and green in summer. Poison ivy is normally found in forested areas and along the edges of forested and open areas. It also grows in rocky areas and open fields. Typically likes full sunlight and isn't very shade tolerant.

Poison oak: The plant grows as a shrub or a vine, with leaves shaped like oak leaves. Also divided into three leaflets. The underside of the leaf is often lighter than the surface and has tiny hair filaments. The leaves also change color seasonally, from bronze when they are unfolding, to green in spring, to red in fall. It is usually found near running water in damp, semi-shaded areas or bright sun.

+Tip: Even if you aren't ultrasensitive to the plants—you don't have an immediate reaction—it's helpful to know what the plants look like. I have knowingly but unavoidably touched poison ivy and poison oak many times. I try to find a creek or water source to wash the contact area, hopefully within 30 minutes. If I didn't know what the plants looked like, I could end up with a nasty rash. But by washing soon after, I have avoided the itchy rash, which can bother you for days. This also prevents spreading the urushiol even more.

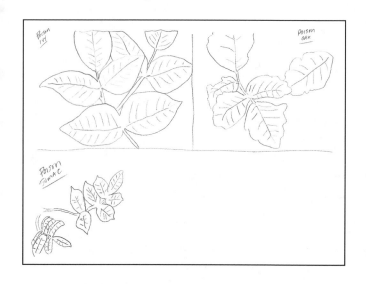

Basically if a plant looks angry, then it probably is not edible.

+Tip: It's an old wives' tale that you can spread the rash by scratching it or by breaking blisters. Scratching can make the rash itch even more, but once you wash off the urushiol, you can no longer spread the "poison."

Poison sumac: This is usually a dense shrub or small tree; the leaves grow in pairs, with typically seven to thirteen pairs on a branch. The leaves are always smooth, and small white or gray berries can hang in clusters from the stalk. Leaves also change seasonally and can be green or red.

Keep in mind that the urushiol (the plants' irritating oil) is not just on the leaves. It's on all parts of the plants, including the bark, vines, roots, and twigs, and can rub onto your clothing, shoes, or dog and later get onto your skin if it is not washed off. Also, it can be released as smoke and inhaled when the plants are burned.

FISHING

After gathering plants and insects, fishing can be a relatively easy way to gain food, and necessary nutrients. Make sure to cook all fish that you catch. There are no poisonous freshwater fish, but the catfish does have barbs on its dorsal fin. Be careful of these protrusions, as they can cut your skin and subsequently get infected.

The simplest way to catch fish is to look for seasonal pools in creeks that may be drying up. This often isolates the fish into these areas and they won't be able to escape up- or downstream. All you have to do is get the fish ashore, and then they are all yours. Sometimes it is easiest to just grab and push them onto the bank, instead of trying to hold onto them. If this is not an option based on the climate of the mountain range, there are a few other ways to catch fish.

First, it is important to be aware of their behavior. Fish tend to feed more heavily before a storm and usually aren't actively feeding after a storm, when the water can be muddy and elevated. Fish will often rest in places with an eddy in an area with heavy currents. They will also congregate in deep pools, underneath brush, beneath undercut banks, or in and around logs, foliage, or other objects that can offer shelter. Fish and salamanders also can be attracted to light at night.

How to Fish

First you will need to prepare a fishing instrument. This can include a wood gorge hook, wire hook, thorn hook, carved wood shank, or a spear point. You can make these in the field out of wood, pins, needles, wire, metal, bone, thorns, or turtle shell.

To make a wooden hook, find or cut a piece of hardwood about 1 inch long and ¼ inch in diameter. Cut a notch at one end for the point and put the sharp object (wire, nail, bone, etc.) in the notch. Securely fasten the sharp object by tying it in place. To make smaller hooks, use smaller material.

To make a gorge, use a piece of wood, bone, or metal. Make it sharp on both ends and cut a small notch in the middle to tie into. You will bait this by placing something

on it lengthwise, so when the fish swallows the bait, it swallows the entire gorge.

The first method, and probably the most straightforward, is to replicate what you would do if you had a fishing rod or fly-fishing setup. Use your cord as your reel and attach bait to your hook or gorge. If you use the gorge method, make sure that your bait covers the entire length of the gorge.

Basket Trap
A basket trap can be constructed using sticks and vines and making them into a funnel shape. You close the top, leaving an opening large enough for the fish to swim through.

Pool or Shore Trap
Gather wood of decent size and length and choose a good location where you can funnel the fish into a smaller area.

FISH BASKET TRAP

OPEN
ENTRY
THAT PINCHES
INSIDE DOWN ON THE
PREVENTING
ESCAPE

This will take some time to construct but makes it much easier to catch fish. Plus, once you have built it, you should have a good source of food for a while.

Spearfishing

Spearing works best in a waist-deep or shallower pool, with larger fish. To make the spear, cut a long straight sapling. Sharpen the end to a point or attach a point made from a knife, metal, or bone. If you don't have a sharp object, you can split the sapling a few inches from the end and insert a piece of wood to spread the area. Then sharpen both sides of the separated halves.

Find an area where there is a fish run or gathering of fish. Place the spear point in the water and move it slowly toward the fish. When you are close enough, impale the fish with a sudden pulse. Do not try to lift the fish on the spear, as it could slip off. Instead, pin it against the bottom

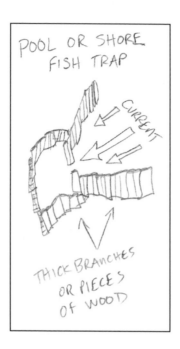

POOL OR SHORE
FISH TRAP

CURRENT

THICK BRANCHES
OR PIECES
OF WOOD

of the stream; keep one hand on the spear and grab the fish with the other hand.

HUNTING

Before you start hunting, you want to make sure that you will be able to kill the animal once it is caught. You can use a rock for this purpose, or you can make a rabbit stick, spear, or sling.

A rabbit stick is a strong stick that is about the length of your arm. You can throw it if you need to, and it can be handy for many small animals that freeze as their main defense strategy.

A spear can be good for fishing and for small game. You want to jab with the spear and refrain from throwing it, as it rarely works when thrown.

To make a sling, put a rock or a few rocks into cloth or fabric and then tie cordage to close off the fabric. Cut the cordage to also create a 2-foot length coming off that you can use to whip the rock and fabric at something.

Birds

All species of birds are edible, although the flavors will vary. If you skin fish-eating birds, they will taste better. Knowing bird behavior will enhance you chance of success. For example, some birds won't leave the nest during nesting season, even when they are approached. Pigeons, and some other species, can be taken from their nest by hand at night. Most birds nest in the spring or early summer. Roosting sites, waterholes, and common flight paths are good areas to catch birds.

If you find a nesting bird, remove all but two or three of the eggs. Make sure to mark the eggs that you have left behind, as the bird will often lay more eggs to fill the clutch. Then you can continue taking the fresh eggs while leaving behind the marked ones.

Mammals

All mammals are edible. As mentioned previously, it will be much more efficient to concentrate your efforts on smaller animals. Keep in mind that all mammals will fight when cornered or to protect their young. Even squirrels have sharp

TRACK PATTERN

WHITE-TAILED DEER
ABOUT 2½"-3"

MOOSE
ABOUT 4½"-5½"

HEEL FRONT
DOG
2¼"-4"

HEEL 2¼" FRONT 2½"
COYOTE

CROW
2½"

TURKEY
4"

RUFFED GROUSE
2"

- TRACKS NOT TO SCALE -

TRACKS WILL SHOW VARIATION DEPENDING UPON GROUND CONDITIONS

TRACK PATTERN

WEASEL
½"-1"

FISHER
2¼"

FRONT 1" COTTONTAIL RABBIT
HEEL 4"

HEEL FRONT
BOBCAT
2"

teeth that can inflict wounds that can become infected. Scavenging mammals, like opossums, can carry diseases.

Amphibians and Reptiles

Most frogs are edible and live close to the banks of waterways. Just don't confuse them with toads, as several species of toad excrete a poisonous substance through their skin. Steer clear of any frogs that are brightly colored or have an X on their back.

Most reptiles are also edible when cooked. You could eat them raw in an emergency since they are cold-blooded and do not carry the same blood diseases as warmblooded animals. Make sure to avoid eating the box turtle, as it largely dines on poisonous mushrooms and can build up toxins in its system.

Most snakes are also edible. See the section on preparation of fish and game for how to prepare a snake for consumption.

BOW AND ARROW

A good bow can take a very long time to make, but you can build a functional short-term bow in a lot less time and replace it just as easily. Find a piece of dead, dry hardwood about 3 to 5 feet long without any knots or branches. Whittle down the large end until it has the same size as the small end. Always scrape from the side of the wood facing you, otherwise the bow will snap when you use it.

Make arrows from the straightest dry wood you can find. They should be about half the length of the bow. Arrowheads can be made from sharp rocks, bone, metal,

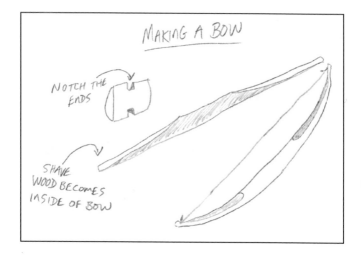

MAKING A BOW

NOTCH THE ENDS

SHAVE WOOD BECOMES INSIDE OF BOW

or glass. Notch the end of the arrows by cutting or filing, so the bowstring will fit in them. You don't need feathers or any materials near the notch, although they will help the arrow fly straight.

To make the bow last longer, remove the bowstring when it is not in use.

TRAPS AND SNARES

If you place several traps, you have the ability to catch more game than one person with a gun. You must be familiar with the animals you are trying to catch and their behavior patterns, and try not to scare the prey away by leaving any signs of your presence.

Look for active areas with obvious signs of runs or trails, scat, tracks, chewed or scratched vegetation, nests, or feeding and watering areas. Make sure to set your traps or snares up without alerting the animal. You don't want to disturb the soil or vegetation in the area, and you might even want to build the components in a different area. Do not use freshly cut or live vegetation, as they will usually bleed sap and this has a distinct smell that can alert animals.

Also make sure to remove the human scent from the area and the trap. It is difficult to remove the human scent, but you can mask it by having mud on your hands. Cover the smells on the trap by coating it with mud or dirt, let the trap season for a few days without touching it, smoke it over a fire, or use the gall and urine bladder from previous kills (do not use human urine). Camouflage the trap after you place it.

Try to funnel the animal toward the trap using its game path. This should be a bit farther from the trap than the animal's body length. Most animals will choose to continue in the direction of travel rather than turning around. The funnel doesn't have to be really thick, just a deterrent to veer from the trail or run. Ultimately the channel should become slightly wider than the target animal's body so that it can't go around the trap.

Baiting a trap increases your chance of success. The animal should know the bait so it draws it to the trap. Make sure that the bait is not also widely available in the area of the trap.

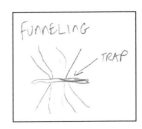

Construction of Traps and Snares

There are a lot of varieties of traps and snares, but the most important part is the trigger. If your trigger is not acting well, your trap or snare will be useless.

A deadfall is a fairly simple trap, with the premise that the animal triggers an object to fall, which thereby crushes or incapacitates the animal. Make sure the weight is heavy enough for the animal you intend to catch. One of the best methods to create a trigger for a deadfall is called the figure 4 system. You will likely have to practice this before you ultimately set up the trap to catch something, as it can be tricky getting the balance right. The system requires notching out three sticks and balancing them in the shape of a 4, as seen in the diagram below.

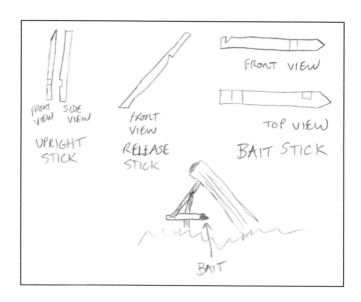

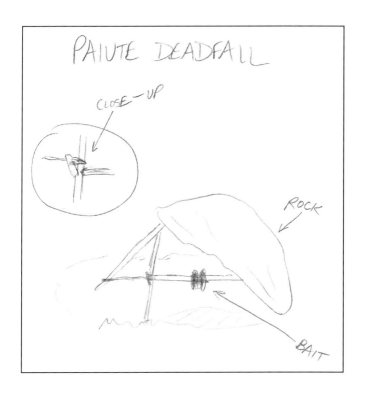

PAIUTE DEADFALL

CLOSE-UP

ROCK

BAIT

It can be easier to balance the system using the Paiute deadfall method instead of the figure 4 system. They are similar but instead of the horizontal stick in the 4, use a small piece of wood tied to some cord. Loop it around the vertical stick in the 4 at a 90-degree angle to prop the cord. Bait the horizontal stick extending underneath the rock. When the animal disturbs the bait, it will release the trigger.

The bottle trap is another fairly simple trap similar to a deadfall. This works mainly for mice or voles. You dig a

BOTTLE TRAP

small hole with an opening that is smaller at the top than the bottom. This inverted opening prevents the animal from escaping. Prop up a rock or tree bark a couple of inches off the ground. The mouse will use this as a hiding spot and then fall into the hole.

A simple snare is one of the easiest systems. It is a noose that is well placed over a run or a den hole and attached to a firmly placed stake. A wire noose is the best option, as it won't slacken. If the noose is made of cordage, you can use spiderwebs, twigs, or blades of grass to help hold it open.

A drag noose is similar to a simple snare but is intended for an animal run. Use pointed sticks on both sides of the run and then lay a stick across the top. Attach the noose to the stick and place the noose so it will be at the animal's head height. The animal will get caught in the noose and pull the cross-stick off the supports. It will then drag the stick, which will promptly get caught up in the other forked sticks that you placed on the side of the run.

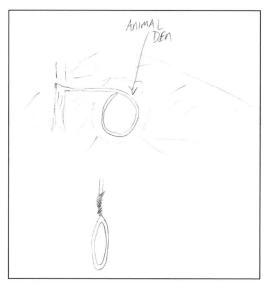

Simple snare

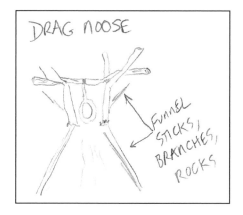

A noosing wand is another method to catch small animals and birds. It often requires a lot of patience, as the user is involved with the process and can't just set up the trap and leave. You want to find a branch or pole as long as you can comfortably handle, and attach a slip noose or wire to the end. You then slip the noose over the animal's neck and pull it tight. Focus on an area outside an animal den or a bird's nest. Use a rabbit club to kill the animal after catching it.

A twitch-up snare is a noose and a trigger to catch the animal. The trigger is typically a sapling under tension that lifts the animal off the ground and creates increased force to disable the animal. Use a sapling with good flexibility and can be bent without snapping. This is a good trap because it can catch an animal traveling in either direction. It works well in conjunction with a funnel to channel

the animal toward the trap. Make sure the trigger is a hair trigger but also able to support the tension of the twitch. Use a stick or branch as the trigger that can handle the tension.

A squirrel pole is a long branch placed against a tree in an area displaying a lot of squirrel activity. Make several nooses along the pole on the top and the sides. Start the nooses about 2 feet from the top and bottom of the pole and fasten the nooses to the bottom. When the squirrel gets

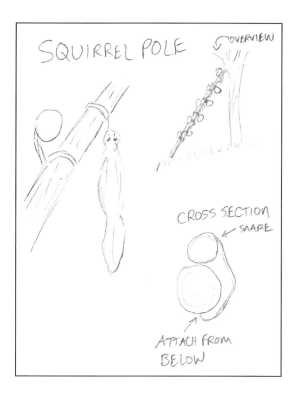

SQUIRREL POLE

OVERVIEW

CROSS SECTION

← SNARE

ATTACH FROM BELOW

caught, it will struggle and fall from the pole and get strangled. You can use more than one squirrel pole in a location to increase your catch.

An Ojibwa bird pole is more functional in open areas near feeding and watering locations. Most birds like to perch above the ground, and that is the beauty of this trap in an open area. Find a straight branch about 5 to 6 feet tall, without any branches and preferably of a non-resinous wood. Sharpen both ends and then cut a small pen-size hole through the top of one of the ends below the sharpened area. Cut a 6- to 8-inch stick so that it is slightly bigger than the hole you just made, and shape it so it barely fits into the hole. Tie a knot in some cord around a small weight, like a rock, about the same weight as the bird species you are targeting. Pass the free end of the cord through the hole and then tie a slip noose to the far end of the smaller perch stick. Tie an overhand knot in the cord and place the perch in the hole. The weight will pull the cord through the hole until the knot prevents it from pulling all the way through. Make sure the noose covers the whole perch and is on both sides. The goal is for the overhand knot to release and allowing the weight to drop as soon as the bird lands on the perch. The noose will then grab the bird's feet. If the weight is too heavy, it could cut off the bird's feet, allowing the prey to escape.

A bow trap is fairly straightforward and is a very deadly trap, so take care if building this. A bow trap is essentially a bow and arrow sitting horizontally off the ground with a trigger or trip wire across the animal trail.

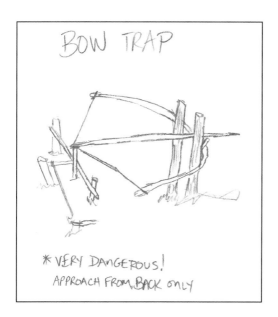

The trigger will send the arrow flying. See the diagram for details.

PREPARATION OF FISH AND GAME

Once you catch something to eat, you must know how to prepare it; otherwise, you will have wasted your time and energy, and will increase your chance of getting sick.

Fish

Do not eat any fish that seems spoiled. Cooking spoiled fish will not alleviate all issues, and this could lead to a serious condition. If a fish has sunken eyes, bad odor, or bad taste, or is slimy or discolored, do not eat it.

Fish must be eaten or cured shortly after catching them. They spoil very quickly in warm weather. Cut out the gills and blood vessels near the backbone. Gut fish that are more than 5 inches long and skin them. You can cook fish by boiling or skewing a whole fish on a stick and roasting it over a fire. The most nutritious way in a survival situation is actually to boil the fish with the skin and then drink the broth or use it to cook something else. You can also smoke fish to preserve it for later. Make sure to remove the head and backbone when curing it.

Snakes

Take extreme caution when trying to catch a poisonous snake. Keep in mind that a snake can lunge rapidly and in any direction. Make sure to pin its head so it can't strike you.

Rattlesnake in striking position.

To skin a snake, cut the head off and then cut the skin down the body 7 to 10 inches. Peel the skin back and remove the entrails. Cut the snake meat into small sections and cook by roasting or boiling.

Other Game

After you have killed the animal, cut its throat and let the animal bleed out. When you make cuts, insert your knife and cut up through the skin to prevent getting hair on the meat. If you are near water, clean the animal. Then place the carcass on its back and cut it from throat to tail, cutting around all sexual organs. Remove the musk glands so the meat doesn't get tainted, then remove the other entrails and the urine bladder, making sure not to spill urine on the meat. If you do so, wash it off the meat as soon as possible.

You can eat the heart, pancreas, spleen, kidneys, brain, tongue, and liver—just make sure to cut the liver open and inspect for parasites. The liver should be a deep

SKINNING AND BUTCHERING LARGER AIMALS

red color. If it isn't, throw it out. Cut the hide from the legs toward the cut you already made in the body and remove the hide. Cut off the feet and head. You can use these as bait for smaller animals. Cut the meat into smaller pieces to transport and cook.

For smaller animals, like squirrels, cut around the midsection, place your fingers under the skin, and pull to remove the hide. Remove the entrails by cutting the body and pulling them out.

SKINNING SMALL GAME

You can preserve meat by smoking, drying, freezing, or salting it. Most of these methods will require you to remain in the same place for an extended period. To dry the meat, cut it into small strips and hang it on a rack with sunny exposure and good airflow. Cover the meat somehow to keep the flies off.

To smoke the meat, you can either build a rack in a tepee shape or have the fire in a hole below ground and a wood rack above. The fire doesn't have to be big or hot—it only needs to smolder so it smokes. Don't let any of the meat touch the fire. If you have the choice, do not use resinous wood. Use hardwood and even slightly green wood, as it will smoke more. Meat smoked overnight should last about a week, and meat smoked a few days should last 2 to 4 weeks.

In cold temperatures, you can freeze or refrigerate the meat to preserve it longer. If you have salt, you can also soak the meat in saltwater to preserve it.

ORIENTEERING, NAVIGATION, AND SIGNALING

FINDING YOUR WAY

There's lost . . . and then there's really LOST. The first lost is more of a temporary misplacement and easily takes care of itself. The second lost is the "I really don't know where I am and may not be able to get back to where I need to be" and is more serious. This is the type of lost you will need help to solve, and you may or may not be prepared for. It's also possible that your maps no longer cover the area you have wandered into or you don't have any maps at all.

What to Do

Step 1: Don't panic! Stay calm; stop and look at the map or topography, using your last known point as a reference. People often consider just one possibility and attempt to make the terrain fit their assumption. Unfortunately, they're often in a different spot than they think they are.

+Tip: Three blows on a whistle is a universal signal for help.

Consider all the possible places you could be on the map. Narrow it down to what fits, using landmarks to triangulate your location on the topo map. You can always retrace your steps to get back on track. If you can determine your location without a doubt, you may be able to figure out a different route to intersect your planned route.

If you're totally lost, STOP. Remain calm and evaluate the situation. Remember, "Undue haste makes waste." Try to remember any landmarks you passed or how long ago you made a turn that changed your course. Can you identify any obvious features (trails, roads, bodies of water, cliffs, changes in vegetation, etc.) that you recently passed? Think about how long you have until dark. If it's going to get dark before you can return to any known points, stay put and set up camp. It's better to set up at a place when you know you're lost than to push on in the dark and get even more lost.

If you're hiking with a group, talk things over and figure out a reasonable plan of action for determining your location and getting back on track. Don't act rashly! If you head out in one direction on a whim and have to backtrack, you end up wasting a lot of extra energy and time, and probably increase your worries.

Step 2: If you need rescuing when you're lost, it can take hours or even days to be found. Help rescuers find you by making a small smoke fire, or, if it's not too much effort, find an open area and lay rocks out in an X or a triangle formation. Also lay out some brightly colored clothes or your pack. Use something that will reflect sunlight onto planes flying overhead or anything else that might help. If you're lost at night, don't camp near running water. The water sounds will make it harder for you to hear voices or people nearby.

If you've called for a helicopter rescue or used a PLB (personal locator beacon), be ready to give details about your, or an injured patient's, condition. Details should include urgency, name, age, sex, and location. If calling, give them your best estimate of location, whether you intend to move, and, if so, where you intend to go. When a helicopter or plane flies over, stand toward it with your arms held in a V

+Tip: ALWAYS leave an itinerary and trip details with people you trust. Ideally, make sure they're in touch with one another as well. When on a long hike, I always give people my planned itinerary and resupply spots. I call or e-mail from each stop to let them know where I am and roughly when they should next hear from me. If they don't hear from me and it's more than a day late, they can initiate the search-and-rescue system, providing an idea of where I should be.

+Tip: I can't emphasize this enough: If you have a map, regularly check your position on it; note where you think you are, and make a mental note of the time you are checking. You'll get to know your pace and where you should be at these intervals. Also check the time at known points, such as bridges, peaks, and other obvious features, as well as road, river, and trail crossings. That way, if you get lost, you will have an idea of how far from those features you've traveled and will have a better idea of where you are on the map.

shape if you need help. If your arms are in a straight line at a diagonal, like a slash, it means "All OK."

If you've managed to find your way before a rescue team arrives, change your PLB signal or call them back to call off the rescue effort. It costs a lot of money to organize and deploy rescue services—and you can be held liable for them. If you do call a rescue service, try to make their job as easy as possible by using the signaling tactics mentioned. This will help your chance of survival and speed up the rescue process.

EMERGENCY NAVIGATION

Without a compass or an altimeter watch, there are a few easy tricks to get your bearings.

①

MARK THE END OF
THE SHADOW.

②

MARK THE NEW POSITION OF
THE END OF THE SHADOW
AFTER 15 MINUTES.

③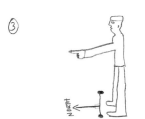

STAND WITH THE FIRST MARK
TO YOUR LEFT AND SECOND
MARK TO YOUR RIGHT. YOU
ARE NOW FACING NORTH.

NORTHERN HEMISPHERE

SOUTHERN HEMISPHERE

SHADOW TIP METHOD   WATCH METHOD

One of the most important tenets of good navigation is checking your location on the map at random intervals and matching your location with the time. This gives you an idea of both your pace and location. Then, if you get off course, you can refer back to the last time you were still on course and have a better idea of where you are because you know where and when you were last on course. You can then make plans to either double back or adjust your route to get back on course. You can also count how many steps that you take in a certain amount of time and then estimate about how far you have traveled by knowing how long your stride is and assuming that you maintain roughly the same steps per time period.

Wear a watch, and know when sunset will occur. If your watch fails, knowing when sunset will occur can still help you figure out what time it is. Cover the sun with your thumb, palm facing you. Each finger above the horizon represents 10 to 15 minutes before sunset.

You can use the sun to tell direction using two methods. An analog watch face's hour hand can help you determine direction, as can a stick in the ground. In the northern hemisphere the sun is due south at noon (it's easier to tell before and after summer, when the sun travels lower in the sky). In the southern hemisphere the sun is due north at noon (again it's easier to tell when the sun is lower in the sky).

When using an analog watch in the northern hemisphere to determine direction, point the hour hand in the direction of the sun, keeping the watch face flat. Halfway between the hour hand and the 12 is south. So if it is 5 p.m. in the northern hemisphere, south would be between 2 and 3. North is opposite that, and west and east are perpendicular. In the southern hemisphere, point the 12 on the watch face toward the sun. Halfway between the 12 and the hour hand is north.

Alternatively, you can place a 3-foot-tall stick, your trekking pole, or something else upright in the ground. Mark the location at the end of the shadow. Wait about 15 to 20 minutes, and mark the tip of the shadow again. Draw a line connecting the two marks. This shows you an approximate east to west direction; you can calculate north and south by drawing a perpendicular line.

Nighttime Navigation

I don't recommend traveling at night when you are lost unless it is truly an emergency. The likelihood of getting increasingly lost or experiencing an injury increases while traveling in the dark. If you travel at night, make sure to take all precautions that you would during the day and more. Try to avoid potential avalanche slopes, but if you must cross them, go one at a time. Take extra care when crossing creeks or rivers in the dark.

Here are some nighttime navigation tricks to stay on track:

- If the moon rises before the sun has set, the illuminated side will be the west side. If the moon rises after midnight, the illuminated side will be the east. This can provide you with a rough east–west orientation at night.

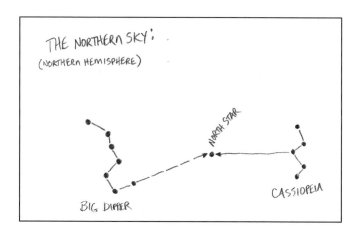

THE NORTHERN SKY:
(NORTHERN HEMISPHERE)

NORTH STAR

BIG DIPPER

CASSIOPEIA

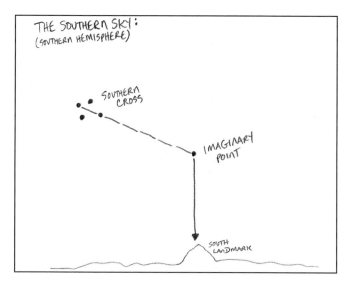

THE SOUTHERN SKY:
(SOUTHERN HEMISPHERE)

SOUTHERN CROSS

IMAGINARY POINT

SOUTH LANDMARK

- If it is a crescent moon, you can draw an imaginary line from the top tip of the crescent to the bottom tip and continue the imaginary line to the horizon to find due south.

- In the northern hemisphere, you can tell north by finding the Big Dipper and Cassiopeia and locating Polaris (the North Star). These constellations and Polaris never set. The Big Dipper and Cassiopeia are always directly opposite each other and rotate counterclockwise around Polaris. The Big Dipper is made up of seven stars, with the two stars forming the outer lip of the Dipper known as the "pointer stars"

+Tip: Try this trick if you can't find a map with distances between trail junctions or the key distances that you want to know. Hold a string to the map's scale, and mark the string to match miles, half miles, and more if you need to. You can then use the string to measure distances on the trail or map, which will give you a fairly accurate measure of distances. Since the trail or path you took or will take is not a straight line, it is hard to accurately measure the distance of a convoluted path without the use of a string. Bend the string to follow the curves of the route, then mark the end of the section that you desire to measure on the string or hold your finger in place. Measure the distance on the string using the map's scale in the legend. This method will give you a more accurate distance.

because they point to Polaris. Imagine a line from the outer bottom star to the outer top star of the bucket, then extend the line about five times the distance between the pointer stars. The North Star will be along this line. Cassiopeia has five stars that form a W on its side. The North Star is straight out from Cassiopeia's center star. After locating the North Star, you can locate true north (the direction to the North Pole) by drawing an imaginary line straight down to the horizon.

- In the southern hemisphere, look for the Southern Cross. It has five stars, and its four brightest stars form a cross that tilts to one side. The two stars

+Tip: It is a common misconception that if you are lost, you should try to follow a creek or river downstream to civilization. This is often not the best approach. In some areas rivers flow directly into the ocean and there is no civilization along the route. In other places the river has carved a canyon with dangerous drop-offs and no possible exit. In the Intermountain West of the United States, many of the water sources eventually flow to inland basins, only to evaporate in the summer heat. A map will dictate what you should do. But if you don't have a map, it is best to get a view from a high point and make your plans and travel path accordingly. Your knowledge of settlements and the specific area you are in will also guide your egress route.

that make up the long access are the pointer stars. To locate south, imagine a distance five times the distance between the pointer stars, and extend this distance from the lower pointer star. The point where the imaginary line ends is in the general direction of south. Look to the horizon, and locate a landmark below this point to act as a bearing.

SIGNALING FOR HELP WITH WHAT YOU HAVE

Here are some options to signal for help:

- Three of anything is considered the universal sign for help. This includes three consecutive blows on a whistle (use two fingers if you aren't carrying a whistle) and three successive flashes from a headlamp or flash on your camera (it helps to be in an open area). Many headlamps now also have strobe features.

- Lay out bright clothes in an open area in a line or a triangle.

- Try using your cell phone to call or text; 911 calls will work on any network. If texting, text your location and condition to your entire contacts list. Save your battery by only turning on your cell phone for a few minutes each day.

- Make a fire in an open area to signal your location, or make three fires in the shape of a triangle. If it is daytime and a fire will be hard to see, add wet

+Tip: When making a triangle or X using any of the above methods, remember that you are signaling to someone in the air. Try to contrast the color of the rocks against the ground. If you are on snow, get dark-colored tree branches or rocks. If you are in a meadow, get light-colored objects. Also make the triangle bigger than you might think you need. The sides should be at least 3 feet wide and 18 feet long.

leaves, green wood, or green vegetation to create smoke and make your fires more visible.

- You can use your cell phone or GPS screen to reflect the sunlight between two fingers. Point the sun reflection at your target and move it back and forth between your fingers to signal.

- Pull a metallic-lined food wrapper tight and reflect the sun's light with it, signaling the same way as above.

- If the ground is snow-covered, pile dark-colored objects, like rocks or branches, in an X shape in an open area on top of the snow. If you can't get to the rocks, you can walk and pack down the snow so it is clearly human-made. When doing this, keep in mind the orientation of the X since ideally you would want the shadow in the trough to be present in the snow most of the day.

If you move to a different location, make sure to leave signs indicating your direction of travel and your planned route.

TRAVEL CONSIDERATIONS AND SKILLS

Generally, in the mountains, people say "follow a river or watercourse to civilization." This is typically a relatively good idea since you will likely have water at all times, and a pretty consistent direction of travel and path for descent into a warmer and more comfortable climate. However, this isn't the ultimate end all, do all strategy. If you have an idea of your whereabouts, this will also play into your game plan. A few reasons following a river to civilization is not always the best option:

- Sometimes rivers peter out in an inland basin, as is often the case in the Intermountain West of the United States or Namibia, and you will likely not come across civilization before running out of water.

- Water courses can be very steep, slippery, and cliff-laden and can lead to added travel woes.

- In some mountainous locations that are prone to flooding or have very steep terrain, like the Nepal

Himalayas, the villages are often on a small flat area, well above the steeply gorged bottom of the river valley. Once the rivers mellow a bit as they descend out of the mountains, you begin to get villages along the floodplains of the rivers, but getting to these areas could entail considerable distance depending on where your situation originates.

Most of the time you will at least roughly know your location or region that you are lost in. If in a plane crash in the mountains, you may have a lot less background. Consider the options and where you are. Evaluate if there are any emergency injuries and if anybody is likely to come looking for you, and if so, how long until they would be notified based on the emergency system in place (e.g., if you are on a hike, did you tell somebody where you are going and if not heard from by such and such a date to contact SAR?). Then build some signaling devices. Determine whether you should stay put based on evaluating your expected timeline for SAR notification and how far/long you estimate you might have to travel to find help.

Figure out which directions are north, south, east, and west. Determine a game plan based on your knowledge of the area, if you have any. For example, in the Himalayas, if you are lost on the southern side of the crest you will be much better off heading down toward the lowlands of Nepal or India to find civilization rather than heading up toward the crest and into a more harsh environment and the sparse habitation of the Tibetan Plateau. If you don't know much about your surroundings, it can be wise to gain a high point so you can gather information and a view of any nearby villages, obstacles you might encounter using various paths of travel, possible food and water sources, avalanche slopes to avoid, and good signaling locations to leave clues in.

In the mountains you may encounter a variety of difficult situations to travel through or across. Here are some skills that will help you mitigate these potentially dangerous situations.

FORDING DANGEROUS RIVERS

Fording a swift river is one of the most dangerous situations you can encounter. You can't always tell a river's depth, flow, or undertow by looking at its surface, and if you get swept down it, your chance of survival can quickly end. Always approach creeks and rivers with respect and caution.

Depending on the size of the crossing, you can sometimes use downed trees to get across without even getting wet. That's always my go-to option if I can find it. My next favorite option is rock-hopping across. Keep in mind that in some rivers, rocks may be glazed with moss, which can make them very slippery. Look for a greenish or brownish color on the upward end of the rock; this can warn you of perilous conditions. Sometimes when the temperature is below freezing, the tops of rocks in a creek can be slick and icy from the splatter of the water. In both of these cases, rock-hopping is still possible, but trekking poles or grabbing a branch to use as a support can be very helpful. So is scaling down the size of each maneuver between steps.

A braided river in the Canadian Rockies with glacial origins. As you can see the water color can be milky and difficult to tell how deep the river is. There is a bar that has been deposited that you can see extends into the middle of the photo. This has shallower water, which you can follow out into the middle of the river and can make the deeper, swift channel much shorter and passable.

General river dynamics are also good to know. Here are a few helpful hints:

- Rivers are deeper under a steep bank and on the outside of a turn.

- They are shallower on the inside of a turn.

- Eddies behind rocks can help break the constant push of the river.

This is a river in Iceland. It is flowing from top to bottom of the photo and shows basic river dynamics. In the bend in the river on the right side of the photograph, the outside of the turn has deeper water and swifter water than the inside. The inside of the turn has a bar deposited, in this case with cobbles, which is shallower. Also you can see a small eddy has formed in the alcove in the center of the photo immediately behind the rock ridge. When you choose a place to cross think about what a stick would do if you put it in the water at that location. This will give you an idea of what will happen to you if you lose your balance and get swept downstream. Sometimes the river may help carry you to the other side. Make sure your egress is easy. Sometimes the banks can be steep, slippery, and eroded.

- Rivers typically meander slowly through meadows, and although the water may be deeper, the current is usually gentler, often making meadow areas safe places to cross.

A braided river in New Zealand with glacial origins. As you can see the water color can be milky and difficult to tell how deep the river is. During times of heavy rain this river can fill the entire valley floor and be completely impassable. At lower flows you can pick areas to cross that are passable since the river braids divide the water flow into multiple channels and separate the volume.

Fast-moving water above the knee can knock someone over. Using trekking poles or a stick is very helpful both for balance and to test the depth of the water and obstacles underneath the surface.

Glacial rivers are sometimes tough to cross because they are silty and you often can't see the bottom. On the other hand, they can also be braided and separated into various paths, helping diminish the intensity of the channel, and the flow can be very diurnal, with significantly less flow in the morning than in the afternoon.

Do not do a tough ford barefoot! Unless the river is really gentle, wear shoes when fording a river. They help with traction and protect your feet in case there are jagged rocks in the water you can't see.

If the river looks too swift and is wide, look for a log across. If that isn't an option, scope out upstream to cross it. Sometimes that means *miles* upstream. But there's often less volume upstream, making the river easier to cross.

When crossing a river, I leave my backpack's sternum and hip belt straps buckled. Some people say you should unbuckle them so that you can get out of your pack quickly if you fall. I have done it both ways, and I find that I really don't like unexpected load shifts when I am in a precarious situation, which can happen when you're not strapped in. So I leave the straps buckled. If I do get submerged, I'm prepared to immediately unbuckle and ditch my pack. Also, I feel that people who say you should unbuckle straps are retelling tales from big, heavy packs or external-frame packs. With a trim, streamlined, ultralight setup, your movements are not affected nearly as much.

If you think someone is going to fall and you have an extra person in the group, you can have the extra person wait downstream. Make sure the catcher has something to help the person get to the shore, such as a solid tree branch, pole, or rope, just in case.

How to Ford a Tough Crossing

Rivers can be crossed in many different ways. While there are other options, the following has worked really well for me in some very tough situations.

Step 1: Scout for a good place to cross the river *before* starting to cross. Rivers are dynamic and change often. Don't just assume that where the trail crosses the river is the best and safest place to do so. Make sure exit and entry points are safe by looking for places where you will be able to ease into the water without losing your balance, stepping precariously, or stepping directly into fast-moving water. Also make sure you will be able to get out of the water without a struggle. Try to pick a spot where there are no visible rapids downstream, particularly with any downed trees strewn across—known as strainers. Getting swept into a strainer is one of the worst things that can happen. The branches dangling off the tree trunk down into the water can catch and keep you underwater and make it difficult or impossible to get out against the force of the rushing water.

Step 2: Take off anything extra that is baggy, like rain pants, that can catch current. Tie your shoelaces and anything else you could trip over.

+Tip: Creeks and rivers rise and fall throughout the day. Often the most difficult crossings are raging from seasonal snowmelt or glacial runoff. If the body of water stems from snowmelt or a glacier, morning is the time of lowest flow and the easiest time to ford. Sometimes the difference is substantial. I have seen creeks rise more than 6 feet between morning and afternoon—basically from fordable to deadly.

Step 3: Sidestep across, without crossing your feet. Sidestepping helps prevent the push of the water from crossing up your legs and getting you off balance. Use your trekking poles for extra balance and also to test the depth of the water. Walk at a slight downstream angle while facing upstream. These tricks will make the river's current more manageable, making it easier to cross and less likely that you will lose your footing.

When Things Take a Turn for the Worse

If you get swept downstream, ditch your backpack immediately and swim for shore, whichever is closer or more manageable to reach. If you are caught in the current, float feet downstream and stomach up, using your feet and legs to cushion and bounce off rocks in your path. The only time you don't want to float in this fashion is when there is a strainer approaching. In this circumstance you want to go head first, stomach down, as though you are doing the butterfly stroke. As you near the strainer, try to lift yourself out of the water by putting your hands over the strainer, pushing yourself up, and kicking your feet. Do this to try to prevent yourself from going underneath it, where you might get pinned.

HIKING ON STEEP SNOWFIELDS

Snow creates unique hiking conditions. Snow conditions can change dramatically depending on recent weather, elevation, and time of year. You can bomb through a dusting of fresh, powdery snow or slog through miles of deep

Use the natural formations of the snow to help you create safe, flat platforms to step on. Trekking poles or a branch used as a staff are also very helpful and provide increased balance and stability, as well as a makeshift ice axe if need be. SHAWN FORRY

powder. Spring conditions are much different and vary throughout the day. Trekking poles or a tree branch used as a staff can be very handy for these situations.

Snowshoes generally aren't worth their weight for spring snow conditions. In spring the snow often has an icy crust in the morning. The crust can be treacherous on steep slopes, particularly when you can't kick steps into it. But it also makes travel fast and efficient. You can often take a shorter, more direct path.

If you need to make snowshoes, you can fashion a pair by tying flexible, green tree branches together into fairly large ovals. Make cross-supports from the outside oval so your shoe will have something to rest on, and then tie your shoe to those supports. This will help create some floatation in deep snow and expend a bit less energy. Progress can still be painfully slow, though.

On winter hikes and in spring snow conditions, plan where you camp and wake up early in the morning to take advantage of the best snow/hiking conditions. This will help you make good time. Traveling in the morning on firm snow will be faster, since you are on top of the snow rather than sinking into it like you will do in the afternoon, when you're postholing and expending a lot of energy in rotten snow. Also, try to walk in shady areas in the afternoon. The shaded snow isn't as rotten, and you won't posthole as much.

Although it is tempting to walk on rocks and get off the snow, keep the following in mind: Snow often melts from underneath, meaning you can sink deeper or even poke through an air pocket under the snow that's deeper than expected. Either take a big step on and off the rocks or give them a wide berth. Also watch out for thin snow bridges with water running underneath.

Take big steps when walking on and off snowfields. Snow is often slushy or punchy near the edges, and those are commonly the first places to soften with daytime warming. Areas that are firm and solid in the morning may require postholing in the afternoon.

How to Ascend Steep Snowfields

Step 1: When you're on snow and don't have crampons with you, route selection is very important. Snow can take the natural contours of the rocks underneath or completely cover them up. In some circumstances, snow can fill in ledges and cliffs and make them scalable. Most important, when you look at the slope you will be ascending, consider two things: (1) If you have the option, ascend someplace with low exposure and low risk if you were to slip and slide down the slope. (2) Look all the way up to your goal. Does the pass have a cornice? Is it overhanging? Are there less-steep areas, rocks showing through, or ledges you can use to help you ascend more easily?

Ascend so that you can attain your desired location to reach the pass/summit. Often cornices are like smiley faces. They are overhanging in the middle of the pass but can meet the ridgeline toward the corners. You can get on top of them without the hassle of chopping steps by simply ascending a bit higher and toward one of the corners. It is not always best to follow the route that the trail would have ascended up the headwall.

Step 2: Since you don't have crampons with you, try to kick in steps on steeper terrain. Spring snow often naturally has little dimples and divots, like a golf ball. Use these natural platforms to your advantage, and kick steps into the snow in these natural depressions. Create a flat area by stamping your foot up and down and moving it from side to side or kicking your toe in sharply on tricky, firm slopes. This helps you get a good, flat position and creates something to anchor one foot on as you craft your next perch. If the snow is softening up, you can easily kick your toe in and ascend straight up the face or kick in the inside or outside of your foot to create a platform and ascend at an angle.

How to Traverse Steep Snowfields

Step 1: Traversing a snowfield can be harder than ascending or descending. Eye the area where you want to go to. It may be where the snow ends, where the pitch mellows out, or where you can see the trail breaking out of the snow. It can be difficult to hold your line across the snow and move perfectly across.

Step 2: Kick steps with the outsides and insides of your feet, making sure each foot is stable before planting to kick the next step. It can be helpful, especially on steep terrain, to traverse at a slightly ascending or descending angle.

How to Descend Steep Snowfields

Step 1: Check your map, and look toward your descent. Pick out landmarks that will serve as guides and keep you on track. For example, go to the right of the first lake, to the left of the second lake, to the outlet of the third lake, on the right side of the creek, and/or below that ridgeline. Since descents can be very fast on snow and you won't be seeing signs of the trail, this will help you find the trail and continue making good time once the snow peters out.

Step 2: If you have an ice ax, you can use the pick end to help control your speed. However, for a lot of hikes, you won't be carrying an ice ax. In these circumstances it can be tricky to control your speed, especially if the snow is still icy and firm. You need to try to traverse to an open area for the descent so that there's less consequence if you slip and speed down out of control. If you can, find an open bowl with a single fall line, no rocks, and a smooth, gentle run-out. Traverse to that area using the techniques described above.

Step 3: If the snow is getting softer, you may be able to safely butt-slide down the slope and stay in

+Tip: The last place snow refreezes overnight is under trees. If the temps are not dropping below freezing or are near freezing, open areas such as meadows and bowls can still refreeze due to radiational cooling. Tree cover prevents long-wave radiation from escaping, keeping such areas warmer. Snowpack is more solid and frozen in open areas and can still be punchy beneath trees. If you are below tree line, look for places where pine needles and plant debris have been deposited in the snow. These areas often stay icier and firmer throughout the day. Also keep this same premise in mind when looking for camping locations, as you will be significantly warmer camping under a tree instead of out in the open.

control. If you are worried about staying in control, you can collapse your trekking pole and use it to help slow you down, as explained below. Another technique I often use when the conditions are softening is to boot-ski down, basically just skiing on the soles of my shoes. It can be really fun but hard to check your speed. You can also walk down fast using the "plunge step" method. This entails stepping down and digging your heels into the soft snow as you descend. You can move pretty fast this way, and gravity helps make it minimal effort. On the other hand, if the snow is still icy, you want to make sure your descent stays completely under control. This can be a much slower process.

+Tip: When hiking in the snow, always consider avalanche danger. Travel in low-angle areas, and try not to walk below steep slopes. Slopes of 30 degrees or greater are more prone to sliding. If hiking in a group through a dangerous spot, move one at a time from safe area to safe area, keeping your eyes on the person going through the treacherous spots.

Travel gently. Don't stand on the edge of cornices or try to break them off—unless you're intentionally trying to see if a slope will slide under the weight.

If you're traveling where avalanche danger is high, take all necessary precautions. Travel with a partner; carry a beacon, probe, and shovel, and know how to use them efficiently.

A sign of increasing instability during the typical freeze-thaw cycle of spring days is when you begin to posthole deeper than your boot top. This means the snowpack is becoming unconsolidated and not

You can wait and take a break if you think the sun will hit the slope and warm up the snow. If there are multiple aspects around, you may be able to traverse a slope that has received more sun and will be softer, or you can just deal with it and pick your way down. Trekking poles can be very helpful. Use the dimples of the snow, and kick steps to create platforms for your feet. Do not try to go straight down; instead, move back and forth across the slope, traversing and creating switchbacks.

bonding or adhering well. In spring, this is usually due to daytime warming and the amount of free water in the snowpack.

In spring, avalanche danger dramatically increases when there's fresh snow. These are usually wet slides, which are slower and start as a point release and spread from there. Rainfall can add weight to the snowpack, and snow is further destabilized from wider changes in temperature during the day and strong solar radiation.

Also, when the snow starts melting in spring, there's typically a lot of rockfall from the added water and freeze-thaw cycles. Stay clear of rock bands and below rock faces.

If you suspect glaciers or see any blue ice, keep in mind the possibility of crevasses. Make sure to avoid these areas at all costs. Without proper safety equipment, crevasses are best left a wide berth.

When Things Take a Turn for the Worse

You tried traversing the steep snowfield but slipped and are heading down the slope, what should you do? You need to self-arrest, but you don't have an ice ax. Here's what to do:

Get your body oriented so that your feet are downhill.

If you are using trekking poles, flip a trekking pole around, as you would if you were walking with an ice ax, so that the tip is facing down. Hold the trekking pole near the tip or at the basket so you don't place too much torque on the pole and snap it. Get the pole so that it is at the base of your neck and your shoulder. Roll your body so it is face

Often there are cornices on saddles and passes. If you are trying to gain the pass or drop off the pass it can be helpful to walk up a little to either side from the actual low point of the pass. Also, cornices can be overhanging and break off, so be careful when walking underneath them or getting too close to the edge. If necessary you can use the adze end of your ice axe or something else solid to chop steps into the cornice.

down, and put all your weight onto the pole tip, digging it firmly into the snow. At the same time, start kicking your toes into the snow repeatedly, one foot at a time. It can also help to crouch your body so that you can get more of your body weight onto your pole and your toes. This should stop you or at least decrease your speed so that it will get easier to stop as you continue these actions.

If you aren't using trekking poles, do the same things as above, but instead of digging a trekking pole into the

Snow can melt out from underneath and be unpredictable. You might punch through into an air space and sink in deeply. Be careful when walking on glaciers, near crevasses, using snow bridges and near rocks, especially in the afternoon when temperatures warm and the snow becomes more unconsolidated.

snow, you will be using your elbow. As you roll over onto your stomach, bend your arm and bring your hand up to your head. Dig your elbow into the snow and put all your weight onto your elbow. Follow the rest of the directions the same as above.

HIKING ACROSS TALUS AND BOULDER FIELDS

When walking cross-country across talus and boulder fields, scope out your route and your ultimate goal on the opposite side. Look for flat areas and rocks to step on. Try not to step in between rocks with narrow gaps. Stash or carry your poles in one hand so you can use your hands and arms as additional points of balance. Using your poles in boulder and talus fields greatly increases the chance of snapping your poles.

WHITEOUTS

If you are in a really bad whiteout, often your best bet is to set up camp and stay put until the weather improves. It is always better to stop early than to continue and put yourself in danger. It is easy to get off track when you can't see, especially if the ground is snow-covered and you can't see or follow a trail. If you have a GPS unit with waypoints programmed in, it can be a great aid to allow

In a whiteout near 17,000 feet elevation. It is extremely difficult to travel in these conditions and try to stay on route.

you to "connect the dots" and keep moving, even though you can't see where you are headed. If you are trying to navigate with map and compass, it is very difficult when you are in a true whiteout.

Before you get lost, set up camp and wait it out. If you think you will be in a potentially life-threatening situation if you wait out the storm, head lower in elevation immediately before it gets too late. Follow a safe course of travel and avoid steep slopes. In big mountains the weather often gets significantly better as you drop in elevation.

INDEX

ABOUT THE AUTHOR

Justin Lichter grew up in Briarcliff, New York, about an hour north of New York City. After college he quickly shunned the traditional career path and lived in southern Vermont; Dillon, Colorado; and Truckee, California, as he followed snow and his passion for skiing. When not hiking, Justin works as a ski patroller. Recreationally he enjoys backcountry skiing, cross-country skiing, snowshoeing, mountain biking, surfing, and anything else active and outdoors.

Since 2002 Justin has hiked over 40,000 miles, including many of the long distance hiking trails around the world. He has also pioneered new long distance hiking routes in multiple countries.

Justin continues to work as a ski patroller in the winter and is constantly dreaming up new adventures.